I0181780

BOXING TAUGHT

THROUGH THE SLOW MOTION FILM

Boxing Taught

THROUGH THE

SLOW MOTION FILM

CARPENTIER	WELLS
BECKETT	LEWIS
DRAKE	BERRY

AND THEIR METHODS

BY

C. ROSE

Author of "Errors That Lose Decisions," etc.

The Naval & Military Press Ltd

Published by

The Naval & Military Press Ltd
Unit 5 Riverside, Brambleside
Bellbrook Industrial Estate
Uckfield, East Sussex
TN22 1QQ England

Tel: +44 (0)1825 749494

www.naval-military-press.com
www.nmarchive.com

CHAPTER I

The Trials and Tribulations of the Embryo Boxer. How Slow Motion Photography will Mitigate them. Where Motion Pictures will Render Invaluable Help.

I suppose it is a fairly safe assumption that the great majority of Britishers over fourteen years of age—and thousands much younger—would like to be able to box with the skill of a Wilde or Driscoll and fight with the craft and force of a "Kid" Lewis.

Hitherto these yearnings have in many cases subsided, or have been suppressed, by hundreds of thousands, owing to the nondiscovery of a royal road to learning the noble art.

Embryo boxers usually have to travel a thorny path before they become proficient. Though they may carry on manfully to the finish and win through, their recital to friends of trials and tribulations encountered during the journey has doubtless damped the enthusiasm of other would-be boxers.

I venture to say that slow motion photography will arouse a new enthusiasm. At first sight it seems a far-fetched notion that a learner may become a fairly efficient boxer merely by practising boxing blows illustrated in this book and seen on the slow motion pictures. But I say here and now that this is quite possible, for one of the best boxers Australia ever produced was Ted Nelson, and he learned to box by practising the various blows in front of a looking glass, and the guards, ducks, and stops for them.

How Slow Motion Photography Will Mitigate Them.

How much easier then should it be for the learner of to-day with slow motion pictures to help him. By their aid he can trace the course of blows from start to finish, and, given an ordinary quantity of grey matter, he should be able to devise plans to intercept similar blows if and when discharged at himself.

I repeat that any reasonably intelligent youngster may escape many of the thorns which have pricked pre-cinema learners, if he studies carefully the blows shown in this book and then follows the example set by the Australian boxer I have mentioned.

It will not be out of place to describe here how "slow motion" pictures are produced. It is something of a paradox to say that an ultra rapid kinema camera is used to take them. This camera takes photographs at the rate of 160 per second, whereas the speed of the ordinary or common or garden kinema camera is only 16 to the second, in which brief space of time one foot of film is used up.

You will naturally ask how it comes about that a picture taken ten times faster than the normal becomes a slow one. The answer is quite simple, as will be seen by the following explanation: *The film is afterwards projected on the screen at the normal speed of 16 pictures to the second.*

I was assured by a representative of Messrs. Pathé Freres that experiments with regard to the slow motion branch of film work are as yet only in their infancy.

Where Slow Motion Pictures Will Render Invaluable Help.

Even as it is, the possibilities are immense. Just think of the many boxing matches which have ended unsatisfactorily by the disqualification, rightly or wrongly, of one of the contestants, for committing a foul. Protests of the boxer and the public alike have, on occasion, been ignored. As a result the best interests of the sport have suffered, and only strong inherent love for our national sport has revived lost interest in it.

These past disappointments would never have been inflicted on us had two cameras, the ultra rapid and the normal, taken pictures of these disputed contests. The employment of the former would speedily have put paid to the account of the get-there-anyhow fighter, the boxer who deliberately fouls on the blind side of the referee and trusts to luck to get away with it. Knowing that Nemesis is on his track, and sure to detect any nefarious practices, this boxer will surely amend his ways beneath the penalty-threatening focus of the ultra rapid camera.

Thus the game will become purer; boxing will be cleaner; in short, the sport, on the whole, will receive a big uplift if the detection of foul play once becomes inevitable.

CHAPTER II

STYLE. HOW TO USE IT. WHY IT CAPTURES THE IMAGINATION. THE SECRET OF THE BOMBARDIER'S POPULARITY LAID BARE. AN IMPORTANT EXTRACT FROM A RULE. HOW TO GET THE GOLDEN EGG. HIS OWN FUNERAL. THE CORRECT WIDTH. HOW TO ADD TO YOUR REACH. WATCH YOUR KNUCKLES. THE OBSERVANT OPTIC. THE ART OF BALANCING. ADVANCING AND RETIRING. HOW TO SPRING BACK WHEN GRADUAL RETIREMENT IS INEXPEDIENT.

STYLE.

We now come to the boxing. Before dealing with the "straight left," which, in the opinion of most experts, is the basic rock on which the science of boxing has been built up, I must say something about "stance," or the position the boxer must assume for attacking or defending purposes.

We will assume that any accomplishment is made much more valuable if "style" is grafted on to it. Take any sport you will, let it be football, lawn tennis, cricket, golf, horsemanship, sculling, polo, billiards, etc., etc., the stylist invariably captures the popular fancy. This is very noticeable in boxing. Take Bombardier Wells as an example. Little else but his inimitable style has helped him to rise

Phœnix-like from the ashes of defeat time and again. Look at the various pictures on pages 41, 43, 49, 61, 63 and 67, showing Wells boxing with Tom Berry, and you will at once grasp what I want to convey to you. On the other hand, it took Joe Beckett many moons to reach his present pinnacle of popularity because he is a rugged workman when compared with the Bombardier. This you can see by turning to page 17. This shows Beckett sacrificing elegance and style in his desire to get in close.

How to Get the Golden Eggs.

On the other hand, Goddard, though he has suffered defeat less often than his two great rivals, will never become a public favourite simply because he has failed to acquire style.

Now as the public favour is a great help to all who gather in its golden eggs, boxers will realise that the cultivation of style is essential. As a fact, the unstylish boxer penalises himself,—as will be seen by a perusal of the following extract from one of the N.S.C. Rules. "*Where competitors are otherwise equal, the majority of marks shall be awarded to the one who does most of the leading off, or who displays the better style.*"

His Own Funeral.

Could anything be plainer? If, in the face of such an explicit statement, the learner neglects to acquire a good style, then it is entirely his own funeral; however, if the instructions I shall proceed to lay down are faithfully followed, then he should reap a golden harvest.

First of all I must lay stress on the importance of standing correctly and holding the hands in the proper position. A correct stance gives not only firmness to the body, but also enables it to be moved about the ring with the minimum of exertion.

The Correct Width.

The left foot should rest flat on the ground with the toes pointing straight ahead; the right foot should be drawn back far enough to secure a firm stand, and the heel should be slightly raised, so that most of the weight of the body is resting on the ball of the foot.

The number of inches the two feet should be apart varies according to the height. For example, if Bombardier Wells's feet were no wider apart than those of a bantam, he would be unbalanced, and thus unable to launch an attack or repel one—unless, of course, he had altered that particular stance. In short, the space between the feet should be just sufficient for your own purposes. One cannot get better illustrations than that afforded by Georges Carpentier in the first picture of the series, which shows him about to lead at Harry Drake.

How to Add to Your Reach.

It is as well not to present too square a front to the enemy. The less you show him to hit at, the more difficult you make his task of hitting you. Therefore, incline the left side of your body to the right and so add a little to your reach. The left arm should be half extended in the same direction, and immediately above your left foot, with the elbow slightly bent, and pressed loosely but closely against the side of the body.

Watch Your Knuckles.

The next item is so important that I shall italicise the words so that they will be impressed on your memory. I refer to the knuckles, *which must face outwards with the thumbs lying along the second joints of the fingers.* On no account place the knuckles downwards or upwards. If you do, you will find out your mistake very speedily and give the bone setters in your vicinity plenty of work to do.

Now place your right arm easily across the *mark*, which vital spot is the cavity which lies just below the breast bone at the point where the lower ribs break off. The safeguarding of this nerve centre cannot be overdone, as a momentary relaxation may result in your finding yourself on the floor with the referee standing above you ticking off the seconds.

The Observant Optic.

Now remains the head. Incline this slightly to the right, at the same time lowering your chin so that the vulnerable point is protected by your left shoulder. Your eyes should look straight ahead when facing an opponent. Rake his eyes with yours, since, with a very little experience, you may thus discover some, if not all, of his designs on you.

CARPENTIER v. DRAKE.

Georges Carpentier in the ideal position for attack or defence.

He decides to lead for the head with his left. Note that as his left travels towards its objective, his right rises towards the jaw to protect against a possible counter.

Drake draws himself together to guard the blow with his right arm. Though he is in an ideal position to counter with the left, he fails to do so.

Here we see the finish of the blow which would have been delivered with the glove closed had this not been an exhibition bout.

THE ART OF BALANCING.

You are now in "position" or "On Guard," and in order thoroughly to familiarise yourself with it, you must practise the following movements until you have overcome the tendency to sway to the left or right, in short, become unbalanced. Lower the heel of your right foot and raise the toe of your left, the effect of the movement being to transfer the greater part of your bodily weight to your right leg. Reverse the movement and repeat until you feel perfectly at your ease. Next step in about six inches with the left foot, taking care to plant the heel firmly on the ground and at the same time transferring your weight to the left foot. Repeat this movement until you feel thoroughly at home, as it will prove to be excellent preparation for the straight left lead with which I hope to deal in Chapter III.

HOW TO ADVANCE AND RETIRE.

However, before initiating you into the mysteries of the blow which has been rightfully described as being the rock bottom of the British style, I shall deal right here and now with the elementary principles of footwork. Later on I shall be much more discursive on this phase of the noble art, since its importance is not to be lightly passed over, simple though it is in actual practice. Therefore I shall touch on only two elements just now, namely the advance and retreat.

To advance, move the left foot forward six inches or so, always bringing up the right foot in support. Do this slowly at first, and gradually increase the speed until you think you have reached your top.

Now try to retreat, which, of course, is exactly the reverse. That is to say, the right foot is first moved to the rear and followed up by the left. Some instructors insist that the left foot should be moved back first, but I do not favour this, as it brings the feet too close together. A possible loss of balance might result which a quick opponent could turn to profit. In my opinion these two cardinal points should be noted carefully and practised assiduously by the learner,—always move the left foot first in advancing, and the right foot first in retiring.

How to Spring Back When Gradual Retirement is Expedient.

There are occasions when gradual retirement, no matter how speedy it may be, will be of little use. Your opponent might make a sudden spring at you with the intention of unbalancing you. To escape him you would have to accelerate your movements correspondingly or stand and meet him. If it is not expedient to do the latter, here is a way out of the trouble. Press hard on the balls of both feet and spring back sharply. If the action is performed properly you will land on your feet in the correct position of "On Guard." Try this movement, and I venture to assert that you will be amazed at the distance you can put between yourself and the enemy.

CHAPTER III

THE LACK OF REALLY GOOD STRAIGHT LEFTS. WHY DRISCOLL RANKS FIRST. WHEN WILDE'S EVASIVE METHODS FAILED. WHY KID LEWIS IS TO-DAY THE BEST LEFT HAND LEAD EXPERT. CARPENTIER'S "SLOW MOTION" LEFT. WHERE EXPERTS DISAGREE. CARPENTIER ON HIS TOES. WHEN AN OPENING IS NOT AN OPENING. AVOID CLINCHING. HOW TO GUARD THE STRAIGHT LEFT, AND MAKE AN OPENING FOR A HOOK.

THE LACK OF REALLY GOOD STRAIGHT LEFTS.

Having become fairly proficient in using your feet to advance and retire, you may now begin to use your hands, starting first with the left. A good straight left is a wonderful acquisition. Curiously enough, though it is supposed to be the chief thing in boxing, the boxers who possess this invaluable asset are extremely few in number. Bombardier Wells, Jim Driscoll, and Johnny Basham have now passed their meridian, but of these three exponents of the left hand theory Driscoll easily ranks first.

WHY DRISCOLL RANKS FIRST.

His timing was at once the envy and admiration of spectators and the despair of opponents. It was an education to see him start a left hand punch later than his opponent and get home first. Jim could beat a man to the punch better than any other boxer I have ever known. Apropos, I once saw him box at a charity show with a leading featherweight. Jim played a merry tattoo on this boxer's face solely with his left hand, and in the dressing room afterwards the boxer was asked how it was—for he was a good class man—he could not stop Driscoll's left glove from connecting. " He never used his right at all," concluded the questioner.

" Don't lead me up the garden," came the reply. " Why," he added, " the way the blows rained on me I thought Driscoll had gloves on his feet as well as on his hands."

When Wilde's Evasive Methods Failed.

Pete Herman, once the World's Bantam Champion, also possessed a splendid left hand. Who will forget that fatal night at the Albert Hall, when he met the World's Champion at a lesser weight,—Jimmy Wilde? Before then, the wonderful Welshman had electrified the whole boxing world with his remarkable ability to escape punches by evasion, and still retain a position from which he could retaliate with lightning rapidity. But he utterly failed to escape the deadly accuracy of Herman's left on that never-to-be-forgotten night.

Why Kid Lewis is the Best of the Present Bunch.

Taking boxers now before the public, "Kid" Lewis comes easily first as a straight left demonstrator. Yea! even Lewis, the murderer; the fierce

JOE BECKETT v. BOMBARDIER WELLS.

Beckett preparing to charge. Note the position of the Bombardier's left hand ready poised to counter.

Wells gets up on his toes and extends his left hand as Beckett gets nearer.

The Bombardier is evidently afraid of missing with his left lead or counter to the face, and therefore alters its direction. He apparently aims at the chest instead as being the bigger target.

relentless fighter; the smashing, dashing, crashing, fighting machine. True, the foregoing does not seem to have much connection with orthodox left hand leading, but my assertion can be proved up to the hilt by going back no further than his first fight with Roland Todd at Holland Park Hall. The Doncaster man is admittedly the greatest defensive boxer of the present day. This opinion has been expressed by all the experts, and gallons of ink have been used up in describing the almost impregnable nature of his defence. How comes it, then, that when once Lewis found fighting was not a paying proposition, and fell back on boxing as being more likely to pay dividends, he jabbed Todd's head back time and again?

I repeat this in the face of Todd's victory in their return match. For though the new middle-weight champion showed improvement in attack and deserved the decision, he did not exploit a left hand lead such as Lewis possesses. It is true that the "Kid" failed to exhibit any traces of its possession during the second fight, but there were cogent reasons why he did not. As they have nothing to do with the argument I will not pursue them.

But I state unhesitatingly, and in full anticipation of an avalanche of adverse criticism, that Roland Todd does not own a straight left which comes within the meaning of the act as laid down by Jim Driscoll. The new champion's leads are the merest flicks. In my opinion they are designedly so, and I think they are employed solely in order to encourage the belief in opponents that Todd cannot punch. They are bitterly disillusioned if, and when, they charge in to run up against admirably timed counters which sting severely. In a long and varied experience of the game I have never seen better.

Lewis is a specialist in that deadly blow, the right uppercut. He brought it off time and again in his fight with "Boy" McCormick, when that boxer was the light-heavyweight champion of Great Britain. He was helped, of course, by "Boy's" lack of speed, but on page 57 you will see that he nearly landed one on clever and fast Johnny Basham. There are three pictures showing the start, the course, and the finish, and these should prove invaluable to the boxer who wishes to cultivate one of the most deadly blows in boxing.

CARPENTIER'S SLOW MOTION LEFT.

Carpentier also possessed a splendid left hand in pre-war days. Of late years he seems to have concentrated on one punch, namely, a swift blow delivered with the right hand, behind which he used to put every ounce of his weight. I have been fortunate enough to get a picture of his left hand in action, and though the blow does not reach its objective, the series of 4 pictures shown on pages 9 and 11 illustrates perfectly the course of the blow from start to finish.

Eight boxing instructors out of ten will tell you that the proper way to use a straight left lead is as follows: From the "On guard" position you step in with your left foot to within striking distance and shoot your glove to your opponent's face. To give force to the blow you transfer your weight from the right leg to the left leg, pressing on the ball of your right foot, which you keep on the ground. This pressure adds snap and speed to the punch.

Where the Experts Disagree.

The two remaining instructors will tell you to spring into striking distance, always taking great care to retain the proper position. However, in the picture shown here depicting Carpentier shooting a left at Harry Drake's face, you will note that the Frenchman's right foot has remained stationary. You may prove this by looking carefully at the spectator sitting immediately behind George's right leg in picture one, and you will see the same face in exactly the same position at the end of the blow in picture four.

Carpentier's position before leading at the face is entirely orthodox. Note the right heel slightly raised from the ground, and the left foot lying flat with both knees slightly bent in order to facilitate movement. It is true that his legs are rather too wide apart to satisfy some of the hypercritical, but then, that may be explained by the fact that few boxers stand exactly alike. Moreover, a boxer's stance and boxing are as much a part of his individuality as his manner of speaking.

No better illustration of this can be afforded than by the picture on the cover representing "Kid" Lewis and Georges Carpentier going into battle in the Olympia ring. Though both of them have been brought up in the school of orthodoxy, neither boxer's style as here represented is strictly according to pattern,—as a fact, the individuality of each is stamped in his attitude.

Carpentier on His Toes.

Here, then, we discover Georges in the ideal position for launching an attack or defending one.

In the next picture we find him intent on attack. His left hand has moved forward and is slightly raised, but the heel of his left foot is off the ground in a way which many sticklers for orthodoxy would no doubt object to. In the third picture it is raised higher still as his arm lengthens, and once again comes in the question of the boxer stamping his personality on his boxing. Though this raising of both heels may be opposed to general principles, there is not the slightest reason to suggest that Georges has not found it efficacious. However, the left leads as demonstrated in actual battle by "Kid" Lewis on page 53, Beckett on page 23, and Bombardier Wells on page 49, are or should be, invaluable to the learner.

Thirty odd years ago there flourished a clever 9st. boxer whose name was Stanton Abbott. When I add the information that he defeated the redoubtable Sam Baxter, and also that clever Birmingham boxer, Harry Overton, who defeated the celebrated Bill Reader, you will not need to be told that he was a first-class man. Well, Abbott seldom boxed with both feet flat on the ground. Nearly always he boxed on his toes, and though the muscle strain must have been great, it doubtless suited him, since he stuck to that style until he went to America, where he was most successful.

On the other hand, many boxers prefer to box on the flats of their feet. Negro boxers are often flat-footed in action, but in their case it is probable that heredity is responsible, since their forefathers did not wear boots, and heels only came into fashion with them comparatively recently.

BECKETT v. WELLS.

The Straight Left.

Beckett does not usually favour straight left hand hitting, but relies chiefly on powerful hooks after getting in close. Here, however, we see him landing on in quite the orthodox style. Note that all his weight has been transferred to his left foot, which is resting flat on the ground.

BECKETT v. WELLS.

A Clinch.

Both prepare to break away.

Wells holding both arms well up and well extended in order to prevent Joe sneaking one home on the "break."

BECKETT v. WELLS.

The Inside Position.

At close quarters. Beckett has secured the inside position and is ready with his left to deliver one or a series of his disaster-laden short left hooks.

LEWIS v. BASHAM.

Holding—on the blind side of the referee. Could Lewis withdraw his arm if he wanted to do so?

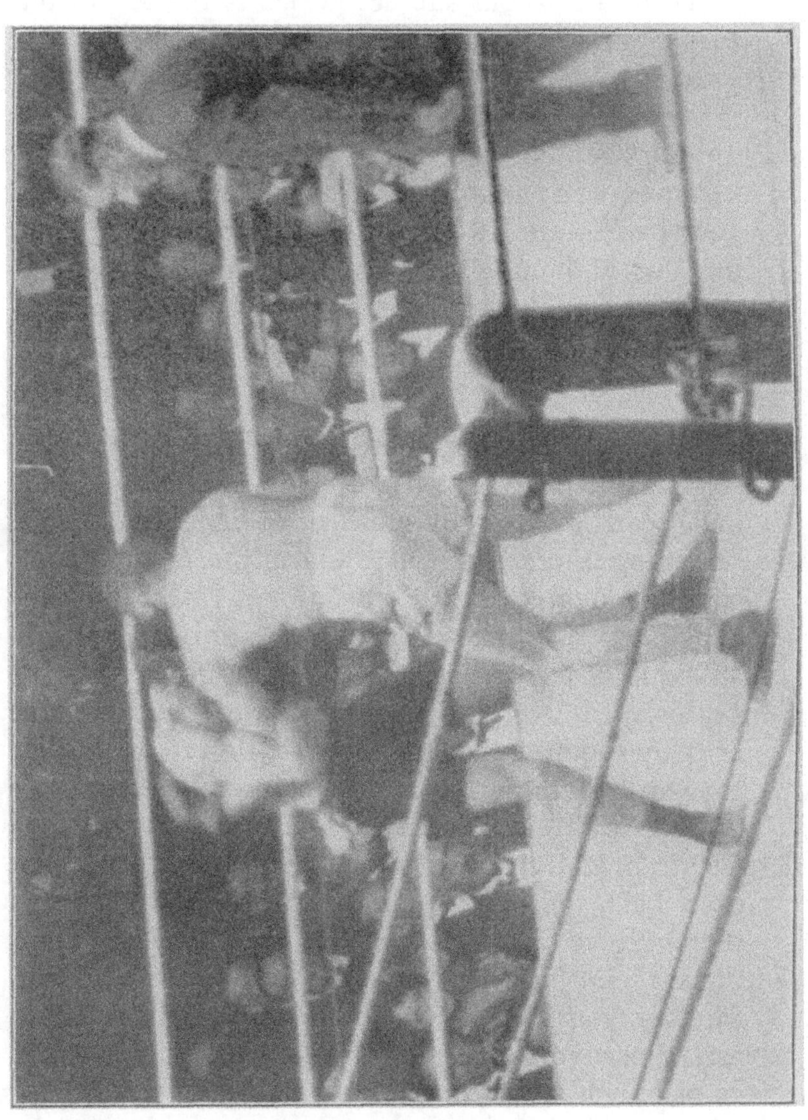

When an Opening is Not an Opening.

To return to our subject, which is the fourth picture, I want you to note how Carpentier's right hand gradually rises as the left glove nears its goal. This is one of the guards for a possible face counter from an opponent's left hand. You will note that Georges' body is uncovered, but if you were to run your hand over his stomach, you would most likely find his abdominal muscles had stiffened up, presenting an adequate defence against a body counter.

Avoid Clinching.

It is rather unfortunate that Carpentier's slow motion left is not one used in actual combat. If it had been you would have been able to see the tautening and tensing of the arm muscles, and the simultaneous closing of the gloves at the moment of impact. But he and Drake are only sparring in an exhibition match, hence the open glove. To be perfectly delivered, the straight left lead to face or body requires that the blow shall land as the left foot touches the ground after being moved from its original position. Only in this way can the full weight of the body be put into the punch. Do not draw back the hand before leading off, as you will thereby give your opponent warning of your intentions. Let it shoot straight out and, above all, whether you miss or get home, spring back again and thus avoid unnecessary clinching. In some cases clinching is unavoidable, and then you should take all kinds of care not to get caught on the "break." The three pictures on page 25 showing Beckett and Wells in a clinch should teach you all that is necessary.

You must remember that it takes two to make a clinch. A boxer with both hands free may punch away *ad lib.*, but too many hold with one hand on the blind side of the referee and punch away with the other. It is very hard sometimes to fasten the blame. Take, for instance, the picture on page 29. Who is in fault in this case?

Now that you have learned the left hand lead to the face you must also learn how to defend it. Get your opponent—I should say your friendly sparring partner,—to lead at you, and practise the following guards and stops.

I need hardly refer again to the right hand guard, as Georges Carpentier has already shown you how to do it, and I will therefore proceed to show you other ways of stopping a left hand lead from landing on your face. With the requisite amount of practice these may be turned to good account. By turning and inclining the head to the right, a left hand lead will pass over your left shoulder, leaving some part of your partner's defence open. If he has raised his right guard to fend a possible counter to the face, his body is open to attack and you at once send in your left. The blow may not hurt because, as I have explained before, the stomach muscles may be tautened against an anticipated assault, but in actual boxing you would score a point, and more glove contests are won on a points basis than by knock-outs.

How to Make an Opening for a Hook.

There is also another method of beating a left lead,—if your eye is quick enough. Chop your right hand across your opponent's left lead as it

BASHAM v. LEWIS.

The Right Lead.

Basham trying a right lead—a dangerous blow to use against an experienced ringster like Lewis. But in this case Basham's audacity would have met with the success it deserved but for Lewis's interposing left arm.

Having failed, Basham drops his right arm across Lewis's left, and thus avoids a reprisal for that hand, whilst keeping a wary eye for Lewis's dexter weapon.

shoots out. This will unbalance him and leave openings for a left hook. Joe Beckett is an adept at using short arm hooks at close quarters. On page 27 he is seen delivering his pet punch on the Bombardier at close range.

Another stop, and punch combined, will be found very useful indeed. I have seen it used but rarely, and the fact has caused me great surprise because it is most efficient. As your opponent leads, throw up your right hand so that you catch the inside of his forearm on your right wrist, and then chop down your right glove on his chin. The blow is quite harmless to look at, but the results are sometimes amazing. The punch travels only a very short distance, but it does not necessarily follow that it is less harmful for that reason. Bob Fitzsimmons,—but I will dwell upon the merits of "Ruby Bob's" right hand hitting in the next chapter.

CHAPTER IV

FITZ'S SIX-INCH PUNCH. THE "KID'S" SHORT ROUTE WALLOP. WHEN TO USE THE RIGHT: NOT EASY TO USE. JEM SMITH'S BODY BLOW. DICK BURGE'S DOUBLE BARREL. SLOW MOTION SHOWS YOU HOW IT IS DONE. PASTE IT IN YOUR HAT. THE ONLY WAY. HOW TO USE THE DOUBLE LEFT.

FITZ'S SIX-INCH PUNCH.

Bob Fitzsimmons was a mighty right-hand hitter, and many of his knock-out punches did not travel more than six inches. The blow with which he killed his sparring partner, Con Riodan, was short in the extreme, and nobody was more surprised than the Ruby-haired one when Riodan failed to recover consciousness.

Sid. Burns, of Aldgate, possessed a powerful short punch when he was in his prime. It was generally a case of curtains when he got it well and truly home. Bombardier Wells could also punch respectably hard when he had once got over the megrims which used to afflict him at the beginning of most of his fights.

THE KID'S SHORT ROUTE PUNCH.

"Kid" Lewis can also hit more than a trifle hard, and though he does not specialise in knock-

BASHAM v. LEWIS.

"Kid" Lewis crossing a left lead from Johnny Basham. Lewis has evidently got home good and hard, as is suggested by the position of Basham's knees.

Basham promptly goes into a clinch, as will be seen from the position of his left glove, while he firmly grasps Lewis's neck.

outs nowadays, in America he often finished his opponents in jig-time. Jimmy Duffy, one of America's cleverest lightweights, twice fell asleep early in the first round. Badoud, the Swiss champion, was also K.O. in a round, while coming nearer home, Frankie Moody and Jerry Shea were "outed" almost before they had begun to fight. All these short route victories were won by short route punches which combined the maximum of effect with the minimum of effort.

When to Use the Right.

While I am on the subject of right hand punching I may just as well deal fully with it. In the opinion of many of the experts the right hand should be kept in reserve until left hand punching has sapped the strength and stamina of the opposition. It can then be used with good results. Much has been written about the right hand cross-counter and its deadly effect. This blow is usually aimed at the jaw or point of the chin, and if it connects fairly and squarely it often scores a knock-out. A lot of force is infused into a right hand cross punch if it is correctly delivered as follows: When your opponent shoots his left towards your face, twist your head sharply to the left and shoot your right hand across his oncoming arm. Even though you may miss his point, because he may have dropped it behind his hunched-up shoulder, you will hurt him wherever you hit him, as truly tremendous weight and impetus is given to your blow by the quick swing of the body from left to right. This is plainly shown on page 37. Here you see Lewis's right glove has reached the side of Basham's head with enough force to make Johnny's knee bend. It is true that the "Kid" has not connected with the jaw, but all the same the blow has apparently hurt.

Not Easy to Use.

Then there is the right lead to the head. This is not easy to use, neither is it safe to employ it against a boxer who possesses a dangerous right hand punch himself. In any case it is very difficult to get it home on an experienced man, as it has so far to travel. Openings must be made for it. Feint in order to draw your opponent's left hand lead, and then stepping a little to the left, you shoot the right straight for the jaw, at the same time keeping a wary eye on his dexter hand, lest he counters you. Lewis shows you how to guard this blow on page 33.

The right hand body blow is also very hurtful. Its effects are often more lasting than those which result from the receipt of a jaw punch. However, in using it, here again precautions should be taken against a right hand reprisal. Still, if you follow instructions you should escape any serious damage.

First draw the left lead; then step in and, ducking to the left, drive your right hand to a spot just over the heart, at the same time throwing up your left arm as a guard for your opponent's right,—if he lets it go. In delivering this blow keep your elbow close to the side and put all the weight of your body behind it.

Jem Smith's Body Blow.

The last of our knuckle fighters, Jem Smith, possessed a terrific punch of this description. He would give his head away and risk getting a punch so long as he could get one of these punches well and truly home. A second application was rarely required. Peter Jackson, the great black boxer, could tell you just how hurtful Jem's right hand body punch was were he alive to-day. The Englishman shot one into Peter's short ribs in the second round of their fight at the Pelican Club, and Jackson almost turned white.

Slow Motion Shows You How it is Done.

One could not get a better illustration than that shown in the pictures on page 43. You will all recognise the tall figure of the Bombardier, who is seen boxing with Tom Berry, of Custom House. Berry has sent in his right hand to Wells's body much in the same way that the old knuckle-fighting champion used to do. You will note in the first picture that Berry's elbow is held close to the side in order to get all possible weight and momentum into the punch. The next picture shows the course of the blow. It is nearly there, and looking carefully you will see Berry's body has swung a little to the left owing to pressure from the ball of the right foot, which infuses snap and force into the blow. Wells has evidently seen the blow coming, and too late makes an effort to counter it, and so detract from its sting somewhat. His left hand is in position to shoot, and Billy does so. It is rather difficult to tell whether or not Berry has ducked the punch, but there can be no mistaking the fact that his right hand has got well and truly home on Billy's ribs. However, a look at the next and last picture suggests that Wells's counter was too late to rob Berry's punch of its sting, since he has pulled his left arm back and dropped it across Tom's forearm in an instinctive effort to minimise its force. But the learner can see from the foregoing illustration how easy it is to stop a right hand body punch if he has divined the intention of his adversary beforehand. The punch has some distance to travel; the striker's right shoulder has to be swung forward, and this takes a fraction or so longer time than the defender would take to shoot a snappy left to the face or shoulder. It is obvious that Wells intended to stop connection by using his left in this way, but was foiled by Berry's momentary burst of speed.

Paste it in Your Hat.

As I have said before, a close study of these pictures will repay the learner. In the first of them you will note that as Berry is ducking to the left in order to take Wells's left over his shoulder, he also has raised his right guard as protection against a counter from Billy's right hand. I cannot stress too much the advisability of taking this precaution. Paste this golden rule in your hat for future reference,—never shoot out your right to any objective without erecting a guard for a possible return from your opponent's right hand.

The Only Way.

Tom Berry's example should be copied by every youngster who wants to rise in his profession.

WELLS v. BERRY.

1.—Berry prepares to deliver a right hand body punch. Note how closely he holds his elbow to his side.

2.—Note the swing of Berry's body to the left and the raising of his right heel, by means of which he gets greater force into the blow.

3.—Wells tries to defend the blow by using a counter, but apparently fails—

4.—since in this picture he has pulled back his left arm and dropped it across Berry's in an effort to minimise the force of the blow.

Though he has had years of experience, Berry has cultivated the habit so carefully that it has become second nature with him, and so strong an obsession that he uses it even in exhibition boxing. As with good habits, so it is with bad. They are easily formed, but very hard indeed to break when once they have established a strong hold. So it behoves learners to practise only the right thing and shun the wrong. In this way only lies success.

Dick Burge's Double Barrel.

The late Dick Burge used to exploit a double right hand punch which I seldom see used to-day. This is the more surprising because the first half of it is far in front of all known feints to compel an opponent to expose his jaw. Dick was an adept at drawing a left lead. Having succeeded, he would incline his head slightly to the left in order that his opponent's arm would go over his right shoulder. Then he would rip his right first into the ribs and then smartly whip it up and over to the jaw. The second punch almost always found the point because the sting of the first punch made the receiver instinctively drop his left arm to cover the stricken spot.

This was a very favourite punch of Dick's. Australian Tom Williams fell to it after having stricken consternation into the ranks of English lightweights by a sequence of sensational victories over several of the best of them.

How to Use the Double Left.

The double left to the body and face is also a much neglected blow which was greatly in vogue twenty odd years ago. George Johnson, younger brother of the more famous Fred Johnson, of Hackney, who fought the great George Dixon, used to employ this blow, or blows, with extremely satisfactory results. He would first tempt his opponent to lead. Having drawn this he would step in, turn his head to the right, so that his opponent's arm would pass over his left shoulder, shoot his left into the body, and then hook it to the face. He had a really uncanny knack of locating the jaw with the second punch, and as his left hand carried a right hand wallop, the fight often ended right then. It is really quite a simple manœuvre, which you can practise with a friend, and quickly become an adept if you persevere.

What Jem Mace Said.

On page 49 we are shown the difference between right and wrong with regard to ducking a left lead. In the first, Berry is seen ducking under Wells's left. No doubt the duck was a neat and clever one, and from a spectacular point of view, most commendable, but it served no good purpose.

That wonderful old-time clever fighter and boxer, Jem Mace, laid it down as an axiom, "never duck without hitting." As Mace was the father of the British style of boxing, his advice should carry due weight, but one need look no further than these illustrations to discover how valuable it really is. It will be seen by the most casual observer that though

WELLS v. BERRY.

HOW NOT TO DUCK A LEFT LEAD.

Note that Berry is too far away to take advantage of the opening with which the Bombardier has presented him.

THE RIGHT WAY.

Berry has slipped his head aside and allowed Wells's left lead to go over his shoulder. Note how this manœuvre has left temptingly exposed the whole of the left side of Billy's body.

Berry has ducked Billy's lead, he is too far away to take advantage of the splendid opening Billy has given him. Wells's once famed "weak spot" lies glaringly open, inviting bombardment. However, one must give credit to Berry for covering himself against a possible uppercut from Wells's right hand, which Billy seems half inclined to use. Now take the second picture. It is true that Berry has ducked without hitting, but note how close up he is and how easy it would have been for him to pummel Wells's body if he had only recalled Mace's advice. The most casual observer will be able to appraise the advantage of the second duck over the first, as they are so admirably shown in the two pictures. For is not Wells's side open and defenceless against Berry's missing right hand attack, while Tom's left side is amply protected by his left arm, as the position of his glove tells us.

CHAPTER V

HIT CORRECTLY. THE NATURAL POSITION. THE DANGER OF HOOKING. THE EFFICACY OF STRAIGHT HITTING. HOW TO HOOK. HOW TO EVADE A HOOK. WHEN VARIETY IS PUZZLING. LEWIS'S FAVOURITE TRAP. THE WELLS WAY OF STOPPING A SWING.

HIT CORRECTLY.

I have previously emphasised the necessity for hitting correctly, that is, with the knuckle part of the glove. According to the N.S.C. rules points are given only for blows which are registered in this way. That is to say, blows landed with the open glove, or with the heel on inside, do not score points. To hit the proper way the glove must be held in the correct position. There is only one way to hold the hand,—that is the natural way. Here is a simple explanation. When your arms are hanging at full length by your side, what is the position of your hands?

THE NATURAL POSITION.

Are not the palms facing your thighs? Exactly. Now raise your arms, extend them in front of you, close your hands, and there you have the natural position. Facing your objective will be the broad, bony surface which runs from the knuckles to the

LEWIS v. CARPENTIER.

"Kid" Lewis gets home with a powerful left on Carpentier's face.

Note the force which the Englishman has imparted into the blow. It is obviously great since Carpentier's head is jolted back with the impact and his knees are sagging.

first joints of the fingers, and if you hit always with that part of the hand you will never be compelled to turn down a job because of broken tools,—provided your bones are reasonably hard.

How often have lucrative matches been reluctantly turned down owing to injured hands, and how often have actual fights been lost owing to the same reason? Any other method of hitting means hospital treatment sooner or later. It is true that you may have seen real champions posturing in photographs with their hands held in other than the orthodox manner, but this may be attributed to the camera man, whose business it is to get something new. This craze for the uncommon is chiefly responsible for the weird poses exhibited on post-cards by boxers, who would never have attained prominence in their profession had they adopted these attitudes in actual combat.

The Danger of Hooking.

A prolific cause of damaged hands is " hooking," instead of straight hitting. Badly timed straight hitting has also been responsible for damage, but mis-hooking is easily first. Why? It is obvious. A hook takes longer to travel, thus its chances of detection are much greater, hence the anticipatory guard,—probably a bony elbow,—more often gets in the way than is the case if the blow travels by the straighter and, therefore, shorter route.

The Efficacy of Straight Hitting.

One can have no better illustration of the power of straight hitting than in the picture on page 53, where " Kid " Lewis is seen landing his left on Carpentier's face. The force the Englishman infused into this punch must have been tremendous, judged by the results as shown. Note the sagging of the Frenchman's knees and the plainly apparent violence with which his head was jerked back between his shoulders. One can wish for no better proof of the efficacy of straight and correct hitting, and it is all the more valuable because we see it demonstrated in actual battle.

However, in spite of all one may say, "hooking" has come to stay. Jimmy Wilde has done much to popularise it, and even that master of orthodoxy, the great Jim Driscoll, has not disdained the use of the hook on occasions. Eddie McGoorty made us familiar with it; indeed, it would not be wrong to say that his left hand hook is famous in every country where boxing is practised. Willie Farrell, known as the actor boxer, has also won many fights by means of a left hook. But he differs from many other boxers in its application, in that while they use the blow at close quarters, or in breaking away from a clinch, Farrell has brought off many knock-outs with long range hooks.

How to Hook.

Delivered in this way, the blow is a most formidable one, and the risk of damage to the hand is also not excessive. In leading off with a hook the elbow is held wide of the body, the arm is bent and kept rigid. To add to its force the shoulder should go with the blow, assisted by a swing from the hips, but above all, remember to turn the knuckle part of the glove toward the objective. If this is not done, a badly sprained thumb will most likely result. The

LEWIS v. BASHAM.

An Upper-cut.

Lewis has drawn Basham's lead, and jerking his head to the left, he prepares to upper-cut with his right.

The upper-cut well on its way. Note how Lewis is drawing his feet together in order to get as much force as possible into the blow.

Owing to Basham's cleverness and quickness of eye, he has evaded the blow by the merest fraction, but look once again at the " Kid's " feet and you will note they are almost parallel.

blow may be used to the body with less risk and, in the case of an opponent adopting an exaggerated sideways stance, it will be found to be very effective.

How to Evade a Hook.

A useful fend for the hooked blow is a downward chop, using your left against a left hook and your right against a right hook. This method of defence is preferable to the step back, since it makes an opening for a counter. However, swings and hooks should be used only in the last extremity, when all other sources of attack have been tapped and found of small avail against the defences of the enemy.

When Variety is Puzzling.

Swinging and hooking are then permissible and may be used profitably. Variety is said to be charming; in boxing it becomes puzzling. To box always on the same lines may easily become a bar to success, whereas variety in style, methods, tactics, and strategy, will surely help a boxer to climb the ladder. If an opponent presents an impregnable defence against straight hitting, you will naturally try to get round where you can't get through. A swing may also be used for strategical reasons.

To "swing like a gate,"—a common boxing phrase—suggests a state of flurry in the swinger, does it not? A flurried, worried, opponent generally presents openings of which the enemy should avail himself. But supposing for the moment that the boxer who is swinging like a gate is "kidding," what then? May not the enemy be encouraged to weaken his defence in his eagerness to take advantage of this supposed weakness, and thus fall into the trap the swinger has prepared?

Lewis's Favourite Trap.

I have seen "Kid" Lewis swing often, especially with his right. To all appearances, these swings have been wild, aimless blows which any self-respecting novice would hesitate to use. But there is craft behind them, and woe betide the opponent who begins to doubt the much-belauded fighting prowess of the "Kid." For that is exactly the frame of mind Lewis has worked and hoped for, and in the fullness of time in goes a straight right which, if it gets home, spells trouble with a big "T."

Now, the non-strategical swinger lays himself open to punishment because, nine times out of ten, he draws his arm back before he lets go. This is an invitation rarely neglected by an opponent who has been taught that the quickest way home is the shortest, and he will shoot out his left to the face or shoulder and arrest the swing in mid-air.

The Wells Way of Stopping a Right Swing.

A capital illustration of how this ought to be done will be found on page 61. Tom Berry has drawn back his right arm preparatory to letting go a terrific swing, whereupon Billy Wells has stepped in and jabbed Berry in the face. If the movement was carried to its conclusion it would doubtless be discovered that Billy afterwards planted his left glove on Tom's shoulder in order to obviate all risk. Wells's pose in this picture is well nigh perfect, and should be copied by all who desire to cultivate a graceful style without sacrificing workmanship.

WELLS v. BERRY.

Wells stops a right swing by a short jab; illustrating the axiom that the quickest home is the shortest. Note that the position of Wells's left arm will prevent Berry's right from landing on the body.

E

CHAPTER VI

WATCH THE SHOULDERS OR BICEPS AND TAP THEM. CHECKMATE. BRAIN V. BRAWN. MENTAL IDIOSYNCRASIES. MASTERLY GENERALSHIP.

WATCH THE SHOULDERS OR BICEPS AND TAP THEM.

A useful method of stopping leads from both hands is to tap either the shoulder, or the biceps, of whichever arm you think your opponent is going to lead with. You can usually discover his intentions by watching his shoulders. At the least sign of movement shoot out your right or left glove, as the case may be, and you will have one less blow to guard. Look at the illustration on page 65 and see how Wells is stopping Berry from using the right, while Billy himself is seeking an opening through which to shoot his own dexter glove. Berry is well covered. His left glove is protecting his jaw, while his right lies across his stomach. In the circumstances Wells can do little but step back and resume sparring in the centre of the ring.

CHECKMATE.

Apparently he does so, since in the next picture we find him in the opposite corner on the same side of the ring with Berry betraying plainly his intention of ducking under Billy's left arm, probably with the idea of shooting his right to the ribs. However, Wells's left hand is poised with the obvious intention of blocking his punch by a tap on Tom's shoulder, while his right glove is in position to deliver an uppercut. But Tom's bony forearm is drawn across his lowered face, hence Billy hesitates, and each having checkmated the other, the next picture shows them gradually straightening up to renew hostilities.

Brain v. Brawn.

Brains play a bigger part in winning fights than most folk imagine. Brawn is all very well in its way, but without brain to guide and help it, the championship goal will seldom be reached. Take the case of Carpentier. Here we have a boxer who was discharged from the French Air Force because he was unfit, and yet he won all along the line in subsequent boxing battles until he encountered Dempsey. On that occasion brain minus brawn was beaten by brain plus brawn.

To be successful a boxer must learn to finesse when fighting. By judicious feinting he ought easily to be able to find out his opponent's weak spots—if any. If his opponent guards the jaw carefully, he makes it obvious to the meanest intelligence that he dreads a punch thereto. Now it would be silly in the extreme to immediately direct assaults on this seemingly vulnerable spot, would it not? What would you do if you were in the attacking boxer's place? The answer obviously is,—go for his body. Correct,—and keep pummelling it until he drops his guard. Conversely, the face would be attacked if it was indicated that the body contained the soft spot.

WELLS v. BERRY.

Wells stopping Berry's right while he looks for an opening for his own. Note Berry's cover, which is well-nigh perfect.

WELLS v. BERRY.

Wells intended to upper-cut, but Berry divined the intention just in time and guarded his chin. The picture is an interesting one, as it shows the moment when Wells realises that Berry has covered and that he must change his plans.

This picture, taken less than a second later, shows that Wells has given up the idea of an upper-cut and is sparring for a fresh opening.

BECKETT v. WELLS.

Beckett and Wells in characteristic attitude, each waiting for an opening. Joe is evidently thrashing out a plan to get past Wells's left hand, which is in position to stop Beckett's rush if and when it comes.

Mental Idiosyncrasies.

Allowance must be made for the mental idiosyncracies of an opponent. If you know that he rarely is able to settle down in the early rounds you will naturally clap on the pace as soon as Time is called, and by thus taking him out of his stride you will advance your prospects of victory. Newspaper experts are helpful to boxers who use their brains. A journalist is observant by training. If he does not know a lot about boxing, save in theory, he is well acquainted with the mentality of the boxers he writes about. In summing up the chances of two boxers he makes allowances for mental and bodily defects, while giving due credit for compensations, hence the thinking boxer may often get a valuable hint.

Not so long ago a fight took place between two well-known big men,—one a splendid boxer, but possessing a temperamental kink,—the other not so good a boxer, but a much harder hitter, and moreover with a brain like ice. The latter,—I will describe him as "A",—was advised that it would be fatal to box the other fellow,—"B." Tons of ink were spilt in predicting "A's" fate if he adopted such a foolish policy, whereas to fight "B" from the word "go" meant sure, certain and swift victory. Well, what happened?

Masterly Generalship.

To the surprise of all the critics, and incidentally that of his opponent, brainy "A" never made the semblance of a fight. He took all that was coming to him with such cool nonchalance as to make the other fellow apprehensive. "B" feared he knew not what. He, too, had read that his antagonist's only chances of victory lay in rushing in, and even as "hope deferred maketh the heart sick," so deferred expectations put the wind up him. He began to fidget. His left hand glove began to flick home, instead of landing solidly as heretofore, while his right, hitherto sent in straight, began to travel circuitously. Right then the other saw victory looming near. He knew that, once his opponent's superior boxing powers were reduced to the level of his own, his greater hitting force must surely prevail. It did, but the path had been prepared for it by as masterly a piece of generalship as I have ever seen, and the boxer who planned it must go far if his other qualities are co-equal.

This is necessarily a very brief treatise on boxing. There are many other valuable phases of the sport I could have dealt with had not space been so restricted. However, I have done the best I could in the circumstances, and I hope and believe that what is written in the foregoing pages will be helpful to the youngster who is anxious to get on. But this I would most earnestly impress upon him,—he will not achieve success without constant practice on the right lines. This way lies the road to championship honours.

A Selection Of Classic Instructive Titles Relating To The Art Of Pugilism & Self Defence In Both War & Peace
Find our entire selection @ naval-military-press.com

ALL-IN FIGHTING

The distilled knowledge of W.E. Fairbairn, legendary SOE instructor in unarmed combat, and inventor of the Sykes-Fairbairn knife, who learned his deadly skills in 30 years on the Shanghai waterfront. Fully illustrated.
9781847348531

ART OF BOXING AND SCIENCE OF SELF DEFENCE

Former Lightweight Champion Billy Edwards shares the techniques and strategies of the sweet science in his beautifully illustrated boxing guide. Explore boxing's transition from bare knuckle spectacle to today's Marquis of Queensbury ruleset.
9781474539548

SELF DEFENCE OR THE ART OF BOXING

Ned Donnelly was a pioneer of boxing training during the late Victorian era. Explore the strategies and techniques used by this trainer of champions via a series of easy-to-follow illustrations and clear, concise coaching steps.
9781474539562

JACK GOODWIN'S BOXING

This 1920's boxing masterpiece by Jack Goodwin puts you in the shoes of a coach in that era. Uncover the best ways to run, manage and train boxers as taught by Jack Goodwin, a champion and trainer of champions in the noble science.

9781474539586

ART OF WRESTLING

George de Relwyskow Army Gymnastic Staff

In the appreciation to this book Captain Daniels, V.C., M.C., Rifle Brigade, states: "In adding a word to this book on the style of wrestling as taught at the Headquarters Gymnasium of the British Army, and having had personal experience in the various holds and throws taught, I consider it has been of great value in the training of the soldier, and the bringing out of those qualities of grit and determination which have been seen in all ranks who have taken an active part throughout the greatest war in history." 1919.

9781783313563

THE COMPLETE BOXER

Gunner Moir provides detailed instructions on the techniques he deployed to become British Heavyweight Champion. Taught in a series of easy to learn techniques, combinations, and boxing strategies.

9781474539609

KILL OR GET KILLED

Rex Applegate's "kill or be killed" helped prepare America's marines, soldiers, sailors, spies and airmen for the realities of war. This highly shared and respected work provides all you need to know about unarmed combat and close quarter engagement with the enemy.

9781474539661

BOXING (V-Five)

The Aviation Training Office of the Chief of Naval Operations

The game-changing V-Five suite of training manuals helped get a generation of American aviators fit for war. Here we explore how the airmen of the US navy trained in boxing as part of their military fitness regime.

9781474539623

THE TEXTBOOK OF WRESTLING

Get your wrestling skills matt-ready from wrestling champion and world-renown trainer Ernest Gruhn. Replete with detailed holds, throws, pins and strategies for success in a wide range of wrestling rulesets.

9781474539647

MANUAL OF PHYSICAL TRAINING 1914

(United States Army)

Published just prior to the outbreak of World War 1, this beautifully illustrated guide was designed to revolutionise the combat fitness and readiness of the US Army covering a wide range of gymnastic and combat calisthenic exercises.

9781474539708

DEAL THE FIRST DEADLY BLOW

United States Department of the Army

This Vietnam-era classic showcases in detail how the US Forces trained in close quarter combat. Known as the "encyclopaedia of combat" it helped a generation learn how to become devastating effective with empty hands, knives and bayonets alike.

9781474539722

HAND-TO-HAND COMBAT

Bureau of Aeronautics U.S Navy 1943

This is one of the best combative manuals from World War 2, developed by the US Navy V-Five Staff, that included the renowned American wrestler Wesley Brown. It is then not especially surprising that wrestling skills predominate in this manual, and form the base skill-set for this combative system.

9781474537391

ABWEHR ENGLISCHER GANGSTER METHODEN DEFENSE OF ENGLISH GANGSTERS METHODS – SILENT KILLING – FULL ENGLISH TRANSLATION

In 1942 the Wehrmacht published a training manual with the goal of countering the "silent killing" tactics used by the British commando units. The manual was – much in line with typical National Socialist terminology -titled

"Abwehr Englischer Gangster-methoden" or "Defence Against English Gangster methods".

This book was compiled due the Wehrmacht intelligence operatives uncovering of a British hand-to-hand course for the SOE, Commandos, et al, on methods of quick and silent killing (undoubtedly developed by W. E. Fairbairn and E. A. Sykes). They correctly assessed that their troops in general and particularly the Geheime Staatspolizei (Gestapo), Sicherheitsdienst (SD), their security guards, and sentries would be in grave danger when confronted by men trained in these methods. This manual/program was the Wehrmacht's response.

9781474538336

HAND TO HAND COMBAT

Francois d'Eliscu taught thousands of U.S. Army Rangers how to fight down and dirty in World War II.d'Eliscu doesn't get the press that Fairbairn and Applegate do, but he did a commendable job writing this book.It is basic, meant for training raw recruits in a short amount of time before sending them to the front, but simple is good when you are in combat, as most combative experts' will tell you.

9781474535823

WE Fairbairn's Complete Compendium of Lethal, Unarmed, Hand-to-Hand Combat Methods and Fighting In Colour

All 844 images of Fairbairn and his assistants can now for the first time be seen in full colour, lending a clarity to the practical methods of mastering the manner of dealing with an assailant, both in time of war and when placed in difficulty during unpleasant modern urban situations. These various holds, trips, kicks, blows etc, allow the average man or woman a position of security against almost any form of armed or unarmed attack.

Captain W.E. Fairbairn would have approved of this new colour version, that gives an illustrative clarity to the original that was lacking in previous monochrome reprints of his work.

All six of W.E. Fairbairn's works in one binding to create the ultimate colour compendium: Get Tough-All-In Fighting-Shooting to Live-Scientific Self-Defence-Hands Off!-Defend

9781783318735

BOXING FOR BOYS

Regtl. Sergt.-Major & B Dent Army Gymnastic Headquarters

A successful system of boxing instruction for large classes, to allow tuition with no detriment to the "backward or shy pupil". Covers Kit-On, Guard-Sparring-Advance-Point & Mark-Ducking-Medicine, Bag-Left & Right Hooks etc. The author considered that boxing systematically taught to the youth was beneficial exercise, and would have a marked elevating influence on the national character.

9781783314607

HAND-TO-HAND FIGHTING

A System Of Personal Defence For The Soldier (1918)

A tough book on the art of hand to hand fighting in the trenches of the Great War. Demonstrating techniques utilised to "do away with the enemy", many of which are barred in clean wrestling, the book includes good clear photographic illustrations presenting important attack methods including the "Hammer Lock", "Kidney Kick", "Head Twist", "Knee Groin Kick", and the "Knee Break", all very important in a man to man, life or death encounter, when fighting in the mud of the trenches.

9781783313983

COLD STEEL

A cold-war combatives classic. John Styers, US Marine and WW2 veteran, lays out his approach to close quarters combat with rifle, bayonet, stick, knife and empty hands. Explore what helped wartime and post-war Marines stay ahead of the competition with lucid imagery and clear combative descriptions.

9781474540643

THE COMPLETE KANO JIU-JITSU

Join world-famous physical culture expert H. Irving Hancock, and Jiu-Jitsu specialist Katsukama Higashi as they showcase the art of 'Kano Jiu-Jitsu' now known as Judo. Get an exclusive glimpse into the transitional era of the martial art, alongside how it uses Japanese physical culture methodologies for self-improvement.

9781474540735

SCIENTIFIC UNARMED COMBAT

The Art of Dynamic Self-Defence

Learn the esoteric Sri Lankan art of 'Cheena-Adi' with R. A Vairamuttu. This guide explores armed and unarmed self-defence drawing heavily from Indian martial culture, alongside wellness and development from Indian physical culture, fitness, diet and medicine.

9781474540728

SELF DEFENCE FOR WOMEN COMBATO

Join the Canadian combatives legend William "Bill" Underwood as he showcases self-defence for women. Over the course of clear photography, sketches and instructions he lays out a curriculum for self-defence for the attacks women would be most likely to face.

9781474540711

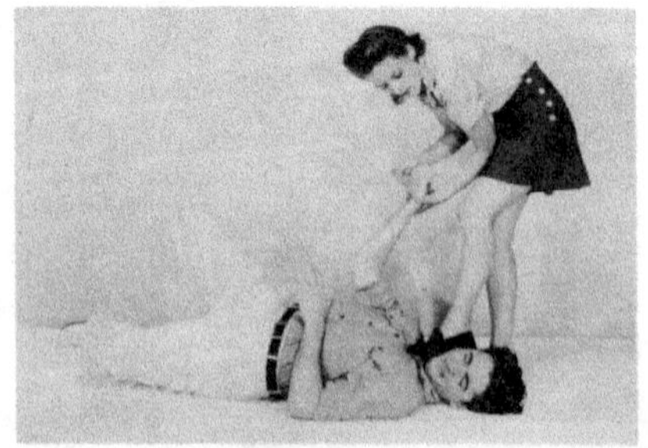

THE NEW SCIENCE

Weaponless Defence

Join wrestling champions Prof F. S Lewis, William V Gregory and Boxing Champ Tommy Burns as they showcase street orientated self-defence from people with a proven track record of fighting success. This 1906 manual via a series of photos and instructions lays out simple, tried and tested ways to keep yourself safe.

9781474540704

COMBAT CONDITIONING MANUAL

Jiu-Jitsu Defence, Bayonet Defence and Club Defence

This 1942 guide for marines lays out the basics of combat Ju Jitsu as part of an overall training regimen for US Marines. It's a holistic guide that covers defences against armed and unarmed attackers, physical fitness and even first aid.

9781474540698

BOXING TAUGHT THROUGH "SLOW MOTION FILM"

Learn the ropes from the best fighters of the 1900s-1930s in this unique boxing manual. Using stills from super slow-mo fight footage, this treasure trove unpacks the skills, tips and tactics of the champs for you to emulate at home.

9781474540681

HOW TO BOX CORRECTLY

Explore the art of boxing according to famous Bronx boxing brand Ben Lee in this 1944 how-to guide. Learn the ropes from one of the nation's top trainers and boxing journalists John J. Romano, in this warmly illustrated guide to the sweet science.

9781474540674

www.ingramcontent.com/pod-product-compliance
Lightning Source LLC
LaVergne TN
LVHW051153080426
835508LV00021B/2611

* 9 7 8 1 4 7 4 5 4 0 6 8 1 *